Original title:
The Comfort of Four Walls

Copyright © 2025 Creative Arts Management OÜ
All rights reserved.

Author: Dorian Ashford
ISBN HARDBACK: 978-1-80587-025-8
ISBN PAPERBACK: 978-1-80587-495-9

Corners of Connectedness

In a space where socks often stray,
And the cat thinks it's a sunray.
Walls that bounce back my loudest cheer,
While the fridge whispers secrets I can't hear.

Chairs in a huddle, gossip they bear,
Crumbs of the past linger everywhere.
Laughter's echo in the cozy spins,
Here's where chaos and calm begins.

Heartbeats in Stillness

In this room, the clock ticks slow,
Tickling my thoughts as they ebb and flow.
Jokes with no audience, just me on the floor,
A dance with dust bunnies—who could ask for more?

A mess of dreams strewn all around,
Echoes of memories make a sweet sound.
Pajamas my armor, no need to impress,
In this snug little haven, I'm boundless, no stress.

Tracing Patterns of Calm

Walls with colors that clash and collide,
Where mismatched frames wear their pride.
Plants that thrive on my dubious care,
And an old couch that swallows my despair.

Piles of books that never get read,
Each a portal to places in my head.
Quirky decor, a charming mess,
Filling the air with whimsical zest.

Domains of Dusk

As twilight tints the room with its hue,
I ponder the chores I never will do.
Sipping tea while the world spins outside,
In the glow of my fortress, I'll happily hide.

The shadows have secrets they share without sound,
Mysteries found in odd things around.
With laughter and quirks, this place feels just right,
Here's where I dwell, from morning to night.

Chronicles of Quietude

In the corners, socks have wed,
Piles of snacks become my bed.
Laughing at the dust that swirls,
Welcome to my land of twirls.

Cats are kings upon their thrones,
Juggling pillows—what a zone!
Here I sip my tea all day,
While laundry plays a hiding game.

Shadows dance with quirky grace,
In this nook, I find my space.
Neighbors think it's all so bland,
But my quietude's quite grand.

My Heart's Room

In my heart's room, clutter reigns,
Old pizza boxes, and some stains.
Walls that echo laughter loud,
In my chaos, I'm so proud.

Giant plants grow wild and free,
Claiming turf just like me.
Pajamas sack my style each day,
Fashion's lost in a quirky way.

Sticky notes that hold my dreams,
And bursting seams that laugh in beams.
It's a raucous little plot,
In this space, I find my spot.

Harmonious Abode

Here the coffee pot sings tunes,
While toast dances like cartoon loons.
Cups is stacked in pyramids,
No one checks what's under lids.

In this haven, socks unite,
As dust bunnies take to flight.
Vacuum timidly crawls around,
Dodging treasures it has found.

Walls adorned with strange collage,
Of memories that make me fromage.
Comfort here is made of weird,
In this nook, no one's feared.

Spaces that Nurture

Spaces where the couch can talk,
Late-night snacks and silly walk.
Walls bear witness to my schemes,
Dreams of reigning with ice cream.

A fridge that hums a lullaby,
While curious cats peek and pry.
Can you hear the giggles play?
In my cozy, wild display.

There's a charm in messy ways,
An orchestra of odd displays.
In every corner, joy ignites,
With each hiccup, we take flight.

Reflections Behind Closed Doors

In a house where whispers play,
Left my socks in disarray.
Cats plot schemes with devilish glee,
While the dog just wants his flea.

Fridge hums secrets of the night,
Leftovers yearn for one last bite.
Mirror mirrors, they all agree,
I should really let my hair be free.

Hearth's Gentle Glow

The fire crackles, sparks a game,
Tell me, who forgot the name?
Marshmallows tossed in a roasting spree,
Watch them melt—what a sight to see!

Blankets piled like a fort on high,
Where myths and dreams no one can deny.
Silly dances in the flickering light,
Hope the neighbors just think it's night!

Nook of Tranquility

In the corner, books piled tall,
Each spine a secret, waiting to fall.
Coffee brewed with a hint of cheer,
Half the cup spills, but hey, that's clear!

Remote misplaced, can't find my show,
Guess it's time for an old radio.
Dancing alone, just me and the tune,
Echoes of laughter fill up the room.

Solace in Shadows

Windows drawn, the world obscured,
Here I take refuge, oddly reassured.
Pajamas worn like a royal crown,
In this kingdom, I never frown!

Dust bunnies hop like they own the floor,
While I ponder what's on the store.
Plenty of snacks, but food quests stall,
Ah, but what matters? I've got it all!

An Embrace from Within

In a room where socks go to hide,
I found a monster under my bed's guide.
Stranger than fiction, it offered its snacks,
Claiming it's cool to watch reruns on cracks.

Walls that listen to every old tale,
Echoing laughter while life sets the sail.
A couch that cushions my giggles and sighs,
In this silly fortress, my sanity lies.

Windows can't judge my dance on the floor,
As curtains flinch at my chaotic encore.
Overturned cushions, a fortress of fluff,
Here I can be silly, never enough.

So I raise a toast to this room where I dwell,
A quirk-filled kingdom where all is so swell.
In every corner, a chuckle resides,
This home brings laughter; it happily hides.

Spaces of Synthesis

The kitchen's a lab for the odd culinary,
Where broccoli battles against jellyberry.
A dance of flavors, both weird and divine,
As I throw in ingredients that simply don't align.

In bathrooms, I ponder philosophical thoughts,
Why do my toiletries gather in knots?
With rubber ducks judging my every mistake,
I laugh at my life, it feels like a cake.

The living room hosts my imaginary crew,
With socks masquerading as slippers for two.
The TV debates what's good, what's bad,
While I snicker, knowing it's all a bit mad.

Each space tells a joke, a story, a rhyme,
Insisting, in chaos, there's order in time.
I roam through each room, with laughter my guide,
These curious havens where giggles reside.

Home's Intrinsic Melody

The fridge hums a tune as it opens wide,
With leftovers dancing, a culinary ride.
A serenade of odors, both pleasant and strange,
Singing sweet ballads in flavor's exchange.

Every creaky floorboard, a voice in the song,
Echoes of mischief, where I quite belong.
Walls share the stories of fall and of trip,
I chuckle at memories, like a comic strip.

Upstairs, my closet with clothes all askew,
Sings loudly of styles, none notably true.
Hats that don't match and shoes lacking pairs,
A fashion extravaganza that laughs at its cares.

So here's to the rhythms of a bustling dome,
Where giggles and gigabytes dance with no comb.
Each note of this melody plays bright and bold,
In a life full of jest, my heart turns to gold.

Pillars of Peace

In my cozy fortress, I sit tight,
With snacks in hand, oh what a sight.
The cat claims the throne, purring away,
While I sip my drink and watch the ballet.

Laughter echoes, the walls all agree,
That my couch is the best place to be.
The fridge hums a tune, a sweet serenade,
As I ponder my kingdom, snacks displayed.

Pillars of cushions raise my flag high,
In my plush domain where worries run dry.
I'm queen of the castle, so regal indeed,
Life's simple joys are all I need.

Through the Keyhole

I peek through the keyhole, what do I see?
A world full of chaos, not meant for me.
Outside there's a dance, the neighbors take flight,
While I stay inside, feeling oh-so-right.

The laundry's a mountain, but I've got my cake,
And a show on the screen, a small little break.
Fuzzy slippers on, I'm ready to groove,
Outside's in a frenzy; I simply won't move.

I hear the wild laughter, it calls to my heart,
But I've got my corners; let's not fall apart.
Through this keyhole, adventures may swell,
Yet here in my haven, all's working so well.

Refuge of the Mind

Within these walls, my thoughts take flight,
With daydreams and musings, oh what a sight.
The world seems so big, but here's the trick,
I can wear my pajamas and still be slick.

A fortress of snacks, where ideas collide,
Do I want a nap, or a movie to bide?
The walls hold my laughter, my quirky delight,
Where whimsy and chaos feel perfectly right.

With pillows for comfort and books close at hand,
I'll travel the realms of my imaginéd land.
So let the outside world spin and twirl,
I'm snug on my couch, in my own little whirl.

The Language of Silence

In the hush of my den, where shadows dance light,
The quiet speaks volumes, it feels just right.
A chair's gentle creak, a soft whispering breeze,
Turned volumes down low, I'm at perfect ease.

The clock ticks in harmony, a comical tune,
As I ponder the mysteries beneath the moon.
A potato in pajamas, delightfully stout,
I embrace this stillness, no rush, just devout.

Here in my bubble, the silence is loud,
No need for grand speeches to make me so proud.
I giggle with glee at this whimsical chance,
To relish in solitude, my own little dance.

The Warmth of Familiar Walls

In a room where socks do roam,
And dust bunnies call it home.
Coffee stains upon the chair,
Yet laughter dances in the air.

Pots and pans in a merry clatter,
What's that smell? Oh, it's just batter.
The walls listen to all our tunes,
Even the offbeat ones from loons.

Crumbs collected like old friends,
Stories woven, it never ends.
The couch a fortress, pillows fortify,
Guarding dreams as we reach for the sky.

So here we laugh, both loud and proud,
In this space, we draw our crowd.
Each wall whispers tales of cheer,
In our haven, there's nothing to fear.

Embrace of Solace

A gentle giggle from the wall,
As cat decides to take a fall.
Plants eavesdrop on every chat,
Hoping we don't notice that.

Our fridge hums songs of midnight snacks,
While lost socks conspire, making tracks.
The clock ticks slowly, teasing the day,
Time assumes a playful sway.

In cozy corners, shadows play,
As we make up games in a silly way.
Each creak of the floor, a comic twist,
In this playhouse, who could resist?

Chasing dreams through the hall, we find,
Laughter echoing, intertwined.
In our bubble, where joy is loud,
Life's goofy moments form a shroud.

Hearth and Heart Unfold

With mugs of cocoa, marshmallows afloat,
Consider all the laughter we wrote.
Tickling toes and playful shoves,
In here, we've built a fortress of love.

The heater hums like an old tune,
Telling of dreams and lazy afternoons.
Board games unleashed where chaos reigns,
Who knew losing could cause such gains?

In the kitchen, a dance of sorts,
With flour clouds and varied reports.
Trying to bake, but ending up in mess,
It's the best kind of culinary stress!

Here's where we trip, stumble, and cheer,
Find our heartbeats all sincere.
Within these walls, our spirits meld,
In this space, pure magic's held.

Enveloping Serenity

Sunbeams sneak through cozy panes,
To tickle our toes and dance on our brains.
With socks mismatched, we strut about,
In our kingdom, there's no doubt.

Chairs squeak softly—a playful duet,
As mismatched furniture cuddles, you bet.
In the corner, a potted friend,
Gathering gossip that we send.

Each knick-knack holds a joke untold,
Stories from the days of old.
In this nest where silliness churns,
The heart leaps, the laughter returns.

Unraveled threads of love we weave,
In this embrace, we truly believe.
With every chuckle, our worries decline,
In these walls, life's perfectly fine.

Hidden Sanctuaries

In a world where socks go to hide,
Behind the couch, they bide their time.
Who knew that space would be their prize,
The arena for a missing rhyme?

Dust bunnies dance in the quiet night,
With popcorn crumbs, they start their show.
The cat presides with regal might,
As they plot fun with the TV glow.

A million stories lurk in drawers,
Old magazines and notes from friends.
Each tiny treasure gently pours,
A tale that never quite depends.

Within these walls, we laugh and cheer,
A kingdom ruled by laughter's art.
No need for grandeur, just good cheer,
Where warm confusion meets the heart.

Gentle Footsteps on Familiar Ground

In the kitchen, chaos reigns supreme,
As I trip over a tower of boxes.
The fridge hums a familiar theme,
While I dodge rogue socks and shoe oxes.

The floor creaks like an old-time dancer,
Each step a song from days gone by.
Caught in a waltz, I lose my chancer,
As the broom declares its own sly lie.

My slippers squeak like silly mice,
As I navigate this narrow lane.
Each turn a twist, yet still so nice,
In this maze of love, I stake my claim.

With every corner holds its charm,
Plants whisper secrets, stuff spills out.
These gentle steps create the balm,
In a home full of laughter, without doubt.

A Quilt of Laughter

Underneath the patchwork dreams,
We gather like unyielding seams.
Each square a story folded tight,
Stitched with giggles that ignite.

A treasure trove of shared delight,
From milk spills to pillow fights.
Jagged edges and cozy ends,
This quilt's a gift from family friends.

When storms may rage and tempests roar,
We huddle close, we want for more.
The fabric of our lives entwined,
Laughing 'til we're all resigned.

With each new stitch a memory made,
Our troubles fade, our joys cascade.
In this embrace, we float and glide,
A tapestry of love inside.

The Unseen Embrace

Four walls wrap 'round, a snug cocoon,
Whispers float on a lazy tune.
A secret dance begins to spin,
In the corners where we dwell within.

Mismatched socks form alliances,
As shoes converse in silent riddles.
Even the spoon joins life's advances,
Creating music with showdown giggles.

The fridge hums a quirky overture,
As leftovers form a secret pact.
Each shelf's a keeper, solemn and pure,
Guarding laughter from the mundane act.

In this realm where joy takes flight,
Comedic stars shine ever bright.
Though unseen, we feel it near,
An embrace of laughter, loud and clear.

The Gentle Crescendo

In a room full of socks, I find my shoes,
The coffee's too strong, I'm feeling the blues.
A cat on the counter, it gives me a stare,
Yet somehow I'm laughing, not a single care.

With crayons on tables, a masterpiece sprawls,
My toddler just giggled, his laughter enthralls.
The walls seem to giggle, the ceiling aloof,
As I dance with the mop, shaking loose all my goof.

Embracing the Obvious

The fridge has a melody, a hum and a tune,
While leftovers waltz, they're gone by next noon.
A towel on my head, I strut like a queen,
Is this artistry, or just being seen?

The clock keeps on ticking, but I'm on my grind,
With a toast in one hand, I'm never confined.
Each wall has its stories, they whisper and tease,
I giggle and snort, in my home of unease.

Behind Each Threshold

Step through this door, but beware all the shoes,
A chaotic ballet where no one will lose.
Cushions are flying, a pillow fight spree,
In my fortress of laughter, all are carefree.

Behind each threshold, absurdity reigns,
With giggles and hiccups, and silly refrains.
The pantry's a treasure, with snacks piled high,
Eating chips by the pound, I wave diets goodbye.

Hushed Harmonies

Whispers of laughter float through the air,
A symphony starts in the couch with a chair.
Popcorn in bowls, as we share all our dreams,
As cats serenade us with their funny schemes.

The curtains all dance to the tunes of our fun,
In this little haven, we're never outdone.
With walls full of antics, and floors coated in crumbs,
Each day's a new giggle, as chaos succumbs.

Within These Boundaries

Here's my fortress made of socks,
A castle built from cardboard boxes.
Walls of laughter, floors of cheer,
Got my snacks and buddies near.

Chasing dust bunnies, we take a leap,
Dodge the chores, escape the deep.
With pillow forts and movie nights,
We dance and giggle until the lights.

Now and then, I hear a call,
'Hey, how'd you manage that big fall?'
I proudly say, with grinning glee,
"I tripped on the rug that belongs to me!"

So here I stay, in laughter's reign,
A jester's heart, dodging the mundane.
Amidst the clutter, I find my bliss,
In this world of wit, there's much to miss.

Spaces of the Soul

Inside these walls my dreams take flight,
With random snacks and silly fights.
A world where socks are never paired,
Yet somehow, no one's ever scared.

The sofa's my throne, a cushy delight,
Where I plot my escape for the night.
The fridge whispers secrets, cold and bold,
Encouraging tales of food to behold.

I play the ukulele, quite out of tune,
Sing of mischief under the moon.
The curtains sway, the windows laugh,
As I take a bow for my one-man cast!

In this snug nook, I can truly unwind,
Laughing loud, leaving worries behind.
With quirky moments and tales to unfold,
These spaces of mine, never grow old.

An Oasis of Stillness

Here I sit, in my cozy nook,
With mismatched cushions and half a book.
A haven for giggles and quirky remarks,
Where my cat rules the jungle and hoards the snacks.

The clock ticks slowly, a lazy friend,
I nap and snack, and then I pretend.
A comedian's dreams swirl in my head,
As I recount the tales from the day I fled!

Oh, how I marvel at the silly mess,
The pizza box sings of my great success.
In funky styles, I wield my charm,
With wall decor, who needs alarm?

So lift your glasses and let's cheer,
To living life without a fear!
In this oasis, chaos looks fine,
Where we mix fun like a perfect wine.

Haven of Heartbeats

Nestled here, with giggles at play,
My fortress of shoes, come out to sway.
The walls can't judge my erratic dance,
As I sprout moves that starve for a chance!

Fridge door swings wide, like a party boat,
With leftover pizza that took an oath.
I share my throne with a rambunctious pet,
Together we scheme, our eyes all wet.

Chasing shadows, we create our scenes,
Crafting laughter from everyday means.
The world outside can wait and pine,
For here, in this sanctuary, all's divine.

We'll pen our stories, wrapped in time,
With quirky escapades that twist and rhyme.
In a haven where heartbeats align,
Life blossoms sweet, like aged red wine.

A Canvas of Peace

In a room where socks are paired,
Cheese puffs sit like royalty,
Paintings lean, slightly unshared,
Living room's pure loyalty.

Dust bunnies dance with flair,
An audience of springtime quirks,
The chair's a throne, if I dare,
Where solitude truly works.

The fridge hums a lullaby,
Mismatched cups take turns to smile,
A pyjama party, oh my!
Laughter echoes through the pile.

Blankets hide my secret stash,
Of daydreams and snack attack,
In this space, I make a splash,
With a popcorn pyramid, no lack.

Walls that Hug

Walls that sway with glee at noon,
Render jokes in every nook,
A sofa singing to the tune,
Of crumbs that fall like a book.

The window winks at passing cars,
While hats hang like old best friends,
Each room's a fading pop star,
Where chaos and comfort blend.

Pillow fights for royal crown,
The vacuum's scared to make a sound,
Every squeaky floorboard frowns,
But it's a laughter battleground.

A snack attack on table's edge,
With chocolate laughing by the cup,
Life's a joke without a hedge,
And here I giggle, never up!

Oasis of the Soul

A space where slippers reign supreme,
And laundry mounts an endless quest,
In every corner, a wild dream,
An oasis that loves me best.

Books are stacked like towers high,
Each spine whispers tales untold,
Cushions giggle, "Don't be shy!"
As I dive into dreams of gold.

The lamp dimly blinks, lights a dance,
While a cat sprawls with regal grace,
Each dust speck waltzes in a trance,
In this cozy little place.

Mismatched socks cheer me along,
With a serenade of tea's embrace,
In my haven, I belong,
Creating laughter, filling space.

An Inner Voyage

Four walls guard my silly plans,
Adventure lives in every crack,
A spaceship made of rubber bands,
Sailing through my snack attack.

Behind closed doors, I'm a king,
With a crown of worn-out hats,
Here, imagination takes wing,
With popcorn and chasing cats.

Each crayon drawing takes a seat,
A map to a candy-land realm,
Pillows shape a trusty fleet,
As I commandeer my helm.

So here I sit, a captain bold,
With a mug full of hot delight,
In my fortress, dreams unfold,
And laughter sails into the night.

Whispering Corners

In the nook where socks do hide,
The cat plans mischief with great pride,
A cushion fort built up so high,
Is where we plot our next great pie.

Dust bunnies dance, a quirky sight,
They twirl and leap with all their might,
Under the table, dreams run free,
As laughter echoes, 'Come, let's be!'

Out of the window, neighbors glance,
At shadows moving, a wild dance,
Within these walls, we're kings and queens,
Creating chaos, bursting seams.

Laundry piles up, a mountain tall,
Here, we conquer it all, after all,
With every giggle, the walls do cheer,
For fun and antics keep us near.

Embrace of the Familiar

The creaky floor sings 'welcome back',
While dust collects in shades of black,
Coffee brews in mismatched mugs,
As we share tales, throw heartfelt hugs.

The clock ticks loud, it thinks it's wise,
But time stands still within these ties,
We ride the sofa in wild spree,
Making up stories, just you and me.

Chips and dip—a grand buffet,
In this realm, we all can play,
With throw pillows flying, laughter reigns,
Against the walls, none bear the strains.

The TV blares our sitcom dreams,
In the pause, we burst at the seams,
With laughter echoing off the walls,
They hold our joy whenever it calls.

Shelter from the Storm

Raindrops tap a merry tune,
Inside, we bounce like a balloon,
The blankets hug in tight embrace,
As squirrels scurry, without a trace.

Cupcakes bake, the oven hums,
While the thunder roars and rumbles,
We play board games, stack the chips,
With every move, we tease and nip.

The windows fog up, we can't see out,
Yet here inside, we laugh and shout,
With snack attacks and silly glee,
A fortress built, just you and me.

The storm may rage, but we won't mind,
In our cozy spot, treasures we find,
With every giggle, we shout, 'Hooray!'
For laughter's sun will save the day.

Quietude in Space

In the corner, a chair stands proud,
While socks and dreams create a crowd,
Television murmurs tales of old,
While we sit snug, joy to behold.

The popcorn flies, a buttery rain,
As we relive that funny pain,
With every slip, a giggle ignites,
In our own world, we reach great heights.

Books piled high, a leaning tower,
Oh, how this space brings such power,
The laughter's glow fills every room,
In our sacred space, scented with bloom.

As clocks tick softly, we plan our pranks,
In cozy chaos, we're giving thanks,
Our laughter shimmering through the night,
In every corner, pure delight.

Beneath a Roof of Dreams

In a house where socks go to hide,
I find my treasures on the side.
The fridge hums loud, a friendly tune,
As I dance 'round spills beneath the moon.

Walls that creak like an old chair,
Whisper stories of my cat's lair.
Each corner holds a snack or two,
Thanking the pantry's magic brew.

The couch is a dragon, fierce and grand,
Where I fight with remote in my hand.
Battles against laundry that won't fold,
In a kingdom both cozy and bold.

My friends all gather, laughter flies,
Pillows tossed like clouds in the skies.
Underneath this roof, we're a crew,
Building memories, goofy and true.

Nestled in Familiarity

In this den, I spill my tea,
Chasing after crumbs with glee.
The cat's my sidekick, firm and stout,
Together we conquer the couch and pout.

Paperwork stacked like a tower high,
And I wonder how it reaches the sky.
Dishes stacked like a daring game,
In this chaos, we thrive just the same.

The walls wear paint, a friendly hue,
A gallery of chaos, oh so true.
With each laugh echoing past the door,
Nestled here, who could ask for more?

Blankets piled high, we laugh and sigh,
Over land of snacks where we lie.
Silly moments, a tangled song,
In familiar nooks, we all belong.

Walls that Hold the Heart

The ceiling's decorated with some dust,
In this fortress, we dwell and trust.
Every phone call echoes with flair,
Between the walls, our stories share.

The fridge is a magician's delight,
Producing snacks both day and night.
Leftovers dance in a wobbly line,
Yet we munch and laugh, feeling divine.

Every corner holds a sock or shoe,
In this nook where dreams come true.
With cushions that swallow us whole,
Here, we gather, we sing, we roll.

Through walls that hold our noisy cheer,
We find our moments, far and near.
Laughter bounces, it simply won't part,
In this humble space that cradles the heart.

Cherished Boundaries

Within these limits, my kingdom sprawls,
Where I can be silly, safe from brawls.
Cozily cramped, my creations reside,
In this space, my whims do not hide.

The bathroom's a stage for dramatic flair,
As I sing to the mirror, without a care.
The living room's set for a game of charades,
With snacks all around, who needs parades?

My office is cluttered, a haven of dreams,
Where I plot out life in glittering schemes.
Lost in my thoughts by the window's light,
These cherished borders make everything right.

We toast to the chaos, we embrace the fun,
In these sturdy walls, our hearts have won.
With laughter and snacks, we brave the day,
In cherished boundaries, we laugh and play.

Sanctuary of Solitude

In my room, I dance like a fool,
The cat gives me looks, thinks I'm no cool.
The laundry's a pile, might start a new trend,
My disco ball's a lamp, let the neon transcend.

Pizza boxes form a new art piece,
Here in my bubble, the chaos won't cease.
Talking to socks, they're my best pals,
Join me for tea, oh, quirky shallows.

Enclosed Embrace

Walls close in, but let's not pout,
I kick the pillows and scream, no doubt.
The fridge hums my tune, a steady beat,
Every snack I grab feels like a treat.

My couch is a ship sailing on dreams,
Adventures await in imaginary streams.
The plants listen close, nodding their heads,
As I share my thoughts on long-forgotten breads.

Refuge in Quiet Corners

In corners, I hide, like a child at play,
The dust bunnies dance, calling me to stay.
I plan my escape to the fridge once more,
While my slippers debate who's keeping score.

Finding a world in an empty shoe box,
Imagining cities made of pizza and clocks.
Each footstep echoes, the walls have their say,
As I laugh with the dust, let them lead the way.

Hearthside Whispers

By the fire, I sit, with marshmallows in hand,
Making s'mores with a fork, my own gourmet brand.
The dog gives a sigh, as I burn the treat,
While he dreams of steak, I'm stuck with this heat.

The sofa's my throne, every seat's a delight,
Cuddled in blankets, a king in the night.
I chat with the shadows, they giggle and tease,
In my little kingdom, I do as I please.

Serenity within the Shelter

Inside my house, I dance with glee,
With slippers on my feet, oh so free.
The cat judges my silly prance,
While I twirl around like I'm in a trance.

Lunch is a feast, leftovers galore,
Hot pizza slice, who could want more?
I wear my crown, a ketchup throne,
In this castle, I'm never alone.

The curtains sway, just like my mood,
Chasing away any hint of brood.
I trip on the rug, my foot takes flight,
Laughter echoes—what a silly sight!

In every corner, a memory stays,
Of lazy afternoons and goofy ways.
The walls hear my tales, oh so bright,
In this snug snugly place, all feels just right.

The Stillness of Four Corners

In my four corners, I sit and munch,
The cereal stays, but I lose my lunch.
The couch is my throne, plush and wide,
Where I reign supreme, in snack-time pride.

The cat sprawls out, stealing my seat,
She snores like a bear—an odd little feat.
I sip my soda, pretending it's class,
But it's really just me, and the cat's fluffy mass.

Neighbors wonder, 'What's that loud noise?'
It's just my dance moves, a parade of joys.
While the walls close in, I'm free as a bee,
In this cozy fortress, just my cat and me.

I count the dust bunnies, total delight,
Each like a friend, in their fluffy flight.
Who needs the outside? I've got my show,
With laughter and snacks, the best place to grow.

Familiar Spaces, Gentle Echoes

In familiar spaces, I make my stand,
With socks that don't match and chips in hand.
The walls are my pals, my trusted crew,
They keep my secrets and my snack stash too.

I often debate with my bathroom scale,
It lies, I swear, 'bout that last night's ale.
Each morning's a struggle, a comedy scene,
Why does breakfast taste different when I'm not mean?

The chair creaks and groans, a song of its own,
While I ponder deep things like why I'm alone.
The walls offer wisdom, or maybe just glare,
As my dance moves outshine their cold, stony stare.

In these gentle echoes, I find my charm,
From silly antics to the warmth's sweet balm.
Though the world outside might seem all aglow,
Here in my smile, I'm the star of the show.

Cradled in Comfort

Cradled in comfort, my fortress of fluff,
A blanket burrito—it's silly, yet tough.
The couch squeaks under my weighty embrace,
While I flip through channels, all over the place.

Pizza boxes gather like friends on the floor,
'Join me!' I shout, 'We'll party for sure!'
The echo of laughter, no need for a crowd,
In my tiny kingdom, I'm throned and so loud.

The fridge hums a tune of delightful delight,
As leftovers wait for a midnight bite.
Each crumb on the counter tells tales of the past,
Good times and silly slips, oh how they last!

So here I'll stay, in this playful embrace,
With socks on my hands—what a silly case!
The walls hold the whispers of joy and of cheer,
In this silly adventure, there's nothing to fear.

The Safe Embrace

Inside this space, I can be a beast,
In pajamas so cozy, I feast on my feast.
With snacks as my shield, I fight off the day,
Who needs to be brave when I'm safe in my bay?

The walls are my fortress, my giggles unfold,
Each corner has secrets and stories retold.
I dance like a fool, no judgment in sight,
In this happy haven, I thrive with delight.

A cat on the couch, he rules the domain,
While I wrestle cushions like they're my campaign.
The clock ticks away, but I'm snug as a bug,
Each tick is a hug, each moment's a shrug.

Outside can be wild, with wind, rain, and lore,
But in here, it's sunshine and laughter galore.
So let the world spin, let the storm have its say,
I'll sip on my cocoa and laugh all the way.

Refuge from the Storm

When thunder roars loud, I snuggle in tight,
Wrapped in my blanket, it feels just right.
The kettle is whistling, my tea's on the way,
I'm safe from the chaos, it's my staycation day.

Out there are sharks in suits—and rain?
But in here, it's a party without any pain.
My couch is a throne, my slippers, my crown,
In this playful kingdom, I never frown.

The forecast may show a tempest of doom,
But I'm laughing with socks like a comedy bloom.
The walls are my buddies, the ceiling my friend,
Together we giggle, this joy will not end.

So let rain tap dance on the roof like a tune,
I'll crank the tunes up and sway to the moon.
With snacks piled high and some nonsense to share,
This refuge of mine is beyond compare.

Tranquil Retreat

In a bubble of laughter and a flickering light,
I wear mismatched socks, feeling pure delight.
The world can keep spinning, I'm not in a rush,
Wrapped in my blanket, I'm feeling the hush.

A dance with the dust bunnies, a song for the wall,
Each sound is a whisper, a sweet siren call.
The fridge hums a tune while I contemplate snacks,
This serene little slice keeps the laughter on track.

With each quirky mug, a smile finds its spark,
I sip my hot cocoa while the dogs start to bark.
The storm might be raging, the weather quite bold,
But here in my bubble, I'm cozy and gold.

So let in the giggles, let joy fill the air,
In this space of pure whimsy, there's no need to care.
An island of nonsense, my heart does a leap,
In this tranquil retreat, my laughter runs deep.

Guarded by Timelessness

Amidst chaotic clocks, I've found my own zone,
Where time stands still, and I'm never alone.
The walls hold my secrets, they giggle and hum,
In this castle of comfort, I've conquered the dumb.

Doodles on napkins, each one tells a tale,
Of marshmallow astronauts riding the gale.
A jester in slippers, I reign over fun,
With each outlandish move, I'm the only one.

The cat gives me side-eyes, he knows he's the king,
As I spin like a whirlwind, he watches my fling.
The wallpaper chuckles as I take a bow,
In this guarded haven, I'm free and I know how.

So let the world wander, let adventures persist,
For in this warm bubble, I cannot resist.
With laughter as currency, I'm rich beyond dreams,
In the safety of silliness, life bursts at the seams.

The Guardian of Memories

In a room where socks go to hide,
A chair remembers when it was a slide.
Last night's pizza awaits, cold and bold,
While the cat, ever purring, claims all that's gold.

Dust bunnies dance in a fog of cheer,
As I trip on a toy that's without a steer.
Old photos grin, stuck in frames of glee,
In this amusing chaos, I feel so free.

A blanket fortress cushions my fall,
With snacks tucked away, it's a grand hall.
Worn-out slippers try to make a guest,
But their aroma? A little less blessed.

Here memories collide in a hysterical race,
With laughter echoing in this cozy space.
As I sip my tea and smile with zest,
This silly abode is truly the best!

Spheres of Safety

Walls adorned with quirky art,
Each frame a story, a wacky part.
The clock runs backwards, time takes a break,
While leaky faucets giggle, for goodness' sake!

Cushions whisper secrets of the day,
As a toaster burns crumbs in its own way.
Beneath these eaves, chaos finds its charm,
Even the broom sweeps with a certain calm.

A fridge that hums tunes off-beat and odd,
Offers leftovers, a gift from the gods.
The windows peek out with a curious glance,
At squirrels that dash in a comical dance.

Here's to refuge, laughter shared loud,
Home is where quirks form a jolly crowd.
Beneath this goofy roof, I take my stand,
In a world of whimsy, oh isn't it grand?

Refuge in the Familiar

The carpet grumbles, old but wise,
As I ponder life's questions and eat French fries.
Curtains sway, with stories to tell,
In a world where my socks misbehave so well.

Bookshelves grin, stacked high with dreams,
Awaiting my journey through whimsical schemes.
A cookie jar guards its sugary loot,
While the couch insists that it's time to scoot.

The kitchen's a playground, messy and bright,
As I concoct dishes that give mom a fright.
Here, silly habits aren't just routine,
But act like the stage for my home-cooked scene.

In this haven of oddities, laughter takes flight,
Sunday pajamas bring joy day and night.
As I revel in nonsense, with a grin so sincere,
I toast to the quirks that keep me here!

Retreat from the Outside

The world outside buzzes with fuss and haste,
But within these walls, I savor my waste.
Here dust is a trophy from days gone by,
And laundry waits patiently, asking me why.

The plants share gossip in pots they adorn,
While I try to decipher what's freshly torn.
A rogue sock ventures, it has no shame,
As I chase it down—such a proud little game!

Outside, they rush with ambition so grand,
Here I recline, a snack in my hand.
The TV debates whether to laugh or cry,
Weighing the options as I just sigh.

So let the world spin in its crazy dance,
I'll take my retreat, seize my chance.
With each silly moment, I find a delight,
In this kooky little bubble, everything feels right!

The Embrace of Safety

Within these bounds, I find my snacks,
A fridge that laughs at diet acts.
The couch is soft, the TV's loud,
In my fortress, I feel proud.

My cat's a guard, more fluff than fear,
Chasing shadows, always near.
The walls listen, they never yell,
To secrets shared, they do so well.

A dance in pjs, I twirl with glee,
These four walls keep wild me.
My trusty chair can hold me tight,
In this haven, I'm a kite.

Who needs a knight when chips are near?
Netflix plays, the mood is clear.
In this great space, I just might stay,
Walls of laughter, come what may!

Walls that Know

My walls can tell a thousand tales,
Of pizza nights and squeaky gales.
They've seen me trip and dance around,
In these corners, joy is found.

The paint's a bit chipped, but so am I,
Like a stubborn fly, we both comply.
The wallpaper smiles at all my woes,
While giggles echo, that's how it goes.

Linoleum floors hold a funky beat,
As I slide around in mismatched feet.
With laughter bouncing off each side,
These walls, my goofy, trusted guide.

In every crack, a memory waits,
Of all the fun, and tasty plates.
Between these walls, we're all okay,
Just hop and skip through life's ballet.

Kisses of Time

The clock ticks loud, but I don't mind,
It's time for snacks, let's unwind.
With laughter slipping through the cracks,
Each moment here, I know it stacks.

Stains of coffee mark my quests,
Adventures chasing all the pests.
These cozy corners hold my dreams,
And silly plans that burst at seams.

Dust bunnies dance like tiny pals,
Their fluff and giggles turn to howls.
With every tick, a wink from me,
In this sweet nook, I'm fancy-free.

The sunlight beams, a golden lace,
In this quaint haven, I've found my place.
Time flies fast but here I'm stuck,
Wrapped in joy, oh what good luck!

Comfort in Companionship

In my little realm, we share our cheer,
With shoes askew and endless beer.
Companions gathered all around,
In our merry chaos, joy is found.

The couch is soft, the snacks are vast,
Between our laughs, our worries pass.
Board games stack in a desirable heap,
In this alliance, friendship's deep.

The plants agree, they nod their leaves,
As we spin tales, no one believes.
With each sunset, we give a toast,
In this warm bunch, we love the most.

So here's to squabbles and wholesome joy,
In our corner, we deploy,
The spirit of fun, forever lasts,
Within these walls, we raise our glasses!

The Caress of Contained Light

In my small room, where shadows play,
The cat's my guard, at least by day.
Snagged on the couch, I hear a squeak,
It's just the fridge, or maybe a leak.

Dust bunnies dance, they trip and fall,
Who knew they'd take the lead in the hall?
I sip my tea, it spills, oh dear!
The walls just laugh, they hold my cheer.

Tangled blankets, cozy and tight,
Who needs a gym? I've put up a fight!
Here's my throne, with snacks in reach,
In this royal realm, I reign and preach.

Outside it storms, the wind may howl,
But here I giggle, hug my towel.
With goofy songs and slippers wide,
This jester's heart, my walls abide.

Walls that Whisper Home.

Four corners quiver with secrets untold,
They giggle softly, like stories of old.
I trip on my shoes, they nod, they know,
The life of a klutz is quite the show!

The echoing walls, they hum and sway,
"When is dinner? Please, not another day!"
The cupboards creak, a voice so sly,
"Got any cookies? Oh, don't be shy!"

Pillow forts rise, they take the floor,
With stuffed animals plotting, I'm never bored.
Together we scheme, against all foes,
Like socks that vanish, where do they go?

Even the clock joins in the fun,
Tick-tock, it teases, "You're never done!"
Yet here I linger, in my nook of joy,
Where laughter bounces, no need for a boy.

Haven of Solitude

In my chamber, I chuckle and stew,
The sock drawer's full, can't find a shoe!
The gleaming mirror? It's seen better days,
Reflecting my dances, my quirky displays.

The bathroom's a stage, I sing in the tub,
Bubbles fly high, oh what a rub!
Each shampoo bottle grins from the shelf,
"Don't worry, friend, we're here to help!"

Couch cushions giggle, they know my style,
As I munch popcorn, I lounge for a while.
Each creaky plank whispers tales of the past,
In this little kingdom, I'm forever cast.

Beneath the drapes, dust motes twirl,
Join in my laughter, give life a whirl!
Time here is silly, like a cat in a hat,
In this secluded space, oh where's my mat?

Sanctuary Within

A safe little bubble, just me and my snacks,
Where thoughts race like hamsters, and laughter attacks.
The walls are my friends, they know my woes,
As I plot my retreat from the world's heavy blows.

Cushions are castles, the sofa a throne,
In pajama regalia, I've never felt alone.
The clock on the wall giggles with glee,
"Let's pause all the fuss, just watch more TV!"

The dust with its flair, it pirouettes bright,
While I swap my worries for pizza tonight.
The laundry spins tales of fabric and fluff,
In this wonderland, oh, we can't get enough!

So here I shall muster my joyful spree,
Among all the quirks, it's where I roam free.
Sanctuary within, what a grand place to stay,
With laughter and snacks brightening the day!

Solace in Shadows

In this snug space, I dance with glee,
My socks on the floor, they challenge me.
Chasing dust bunnies, what a delight,
Who knew that boredom could take flight?

With a blanket fort, I reach for the stars,
Imagination soaring, no need for cars.
A kingdom of cushions, I rule the roost,
The dog's my knight, together we boost!

The chair squeaks a song, just for my ears,
A laughter-filled fortress, away from fears.
Echoes of giggles bounce off the walls,
In my cozy retreat, joy ultimately calls.

As snacks pile high, I grin and delight,
Rediscovering fun, from morning to night.
With mischief around, the shadows convene,
In this silly castle, I reign as queen!

Embracing the Intimate

In a nook so charming, we share a chair,
You with your knitting, I pretend to care.
The cat's on your lap, as warm as can be,
While I sip my tea, plotting mischief at three.

Pajamas, the crown of our reign at home,
With crumbs on the couch, we explore and roam.
A Pictionary game turns into a brawl,
Where doodles become our best comedic thrall.

Even the fridge joins our laugh-out-loud spree,
With leftovers dancing, just savory glee.
In our private world, where silence is gold,
The funny unfolds, as our secrets unfold.

Who needs the outside? We've got our own fun,
With tickles and tales until day is done.
In this perfect bubble, all chaos feels bright,
Like a sitcom replayed, there's joy in the flight!

A Haven from the World

Here in my room, the outside does fade,
With cushions for pillows, it's quite the charade.
I build up my walls with laughter and snacks,
While time takes a breather, no worries, just laughs.

The clock's ticking slow, like a cat on a perch,
No rush to escape, this is my quirky church.
Where the couch becomes throne, my reign's well defined,
With laughs as my scepter, and silliness blind.

Remote in my hand, I change the whole show,
From drama to comedy, let good times flow.
The neighbor's dog barks, but it's just serenade,
As we lose ourselves deep in the charade.

With each giggle shared, a fortress we build,
Against all the noise, every fear is distilled.
In this funny sanctuary, I rest my head,
Laughing as worries dance lightly and spread!

Cozy Echoes of Home

In cozy corners, the echoes all play,
With laughter bouncing in the silliest way.
The cat sauce whirs as I stifle a grin,
Each giggle a spark, bringing warmth from within.

Socks throw a party, mismatched and loud,
As I trip over pillows, feeling quite proud.
The walls hold our secrets and giggles galore,
In a symphony soft, life's joy we explore.

Popcorn explosions in movies we love,
With snorts when we laugh, like gifts from above.
The doorbell's a monster, we jump with a shriek,
While hiding our snacks, it's laughter we seek.

So cheers to the moments, so quirky and bright,
In our warm little bubble, we soar to new heights.
With mischief and fun, love fills every space,
In my happy escape, every heart finds its place!

Refuge of the Heart

Inside these walls, where socks do roam,
Pillows host a party, oh what a home!
Cats claim the couch, like it's their throne,
While the microwave sings a dinner-time tone.

The fridge is a treasure, oh what a score,
Last night's leftovers beg me to explore.
With takeout menus piled on the chair,
Who needs a chef? We've got takeout flair!

Jokes bounce off the walls, like rubbery balls,
Each laugh ignites joy, as mischief enthralls.
The dog steals my sandwich, with a cheeky grin,
And who knew my slippers could spark such a win!

So here we gather, in chaos and glee,
With love in the air, as wild as can be.
Home isn't just where the heart finds its beat,
It's also where laughter and snacks are a treat!

Abode of Serenity

In a haven of chaos, we find our retreat,
Where the laundry piles high, oh so neat.
The coffee pot brews, whispering sweet songs,
While socks play hide-and-seek, righting the wrongs.

A couch with crumbs, a blanket fort tall,
This is the kingdom; we rule over all.
Dinner is chaos, those pots really clank,
Yet love fills the air, and we give thanks.

We dance in the kitchen, with spoons as our mic,
While the cat gives us looks, oh, what a strike!
Can't find my keys? They must have a dream,
Hiding in pockets, or a sweater's seam.

Four walls that embrace, through thick and through thin,
A place where the laughter always begins.
In this sweet abode, so cozy and fun,
Our hearts find a home, as bright as the sun.

Echoes of Laughter

These walls hear the echoes of giggles and glee,
As we stumble through dances, wild and free.
The coffee spills, oh what a sight,
As we laugh at our chaos into the night.

A game of charades, where no one can guess,
With hand-gestures flying, it's anyone's mess!
"Is that a pickle?" a voice calls from the floor,
"Or did we just take this too far once more?"

Pajama parties where we snack as we talk,
While crafting tall tales on our nightly walk.
The walls seem to giggle, they join in the fun,
"Just another day, let's see what's begun!"

So here we gather, a rowdy brigade,
With laughter and love, our fond memories made.
In this joyful place, with mischief at hand,
We dance through the chaos, a whimsical band!

Sanctuary of Togetherness

In a castle built from laughter and snacks,
We find our bliss, no need for artifacts.
The couch is our throne, where legends are spun,
Over popcorn battles, our hearts always run.

With board games scattered across the floor,
Who knew such rivalry could unlock the door?
"This is my territory," declares the old chair,
While the cat holds court, with a regal air.

Temporary chaos, all part of the plan,
As we giggle at life, just the way that we can.
"Who left the milk out?" rings through the air,
As we trip on the shoes that someone laid bare.

So here's to our walls, that promise a tale,
Of snorts, silly faces, and heartwarming wails.
In a sanctuary bright, we all belong,
With bonds that remind us, together we're strong!

Where Silence Speaks

Inside my cozy room, jokes take flight,
Even the dust bunnies dance with delight.
I trip over shoes, a comedy show,
Laughter echoes softly, it's the star of the show.

Coffee spills on my favorite chair,
I giggle at the stains, oh what a dare!
The cat's plotting schemes, I swear she's shrewd,
In this tiny arena, I'm not the only goof.

The Nesting Place

Pajamas as armor, I conquer the day,
Socks mismatched, but they're here to stay.
In my fortress of snacks, a castle so grand,
I rule from my pillow, with snacks close at hand.

Spiders spin webs, set a cordial trap,
I invite them for tea, it's quite the mishap.
Beneath blankets piled, I vanish from sight,
Such a nesting place, where wrong feels so right.

Tranquil Embrace

A couch potato throne, cushions surrounding,
In a still sanctuary, my laughter resounding.
The plant in the corner has seen better days,
   We share our jokes in this quirky maze.

The fridge hums a tune, it's a sweet serenade,
   While leftovers whisper, 'Don't be afraid!'
I dance with the mop, she knows all my steps,
This tranquil embrace is where nonsense preps.

Walls of Warmth

Walls closing in? No, they're giving me hugs,
Embracing my chaos, like old silly mugs.
I jabber to walls, they nod and they grin,
In this space full of laughter, I always win.

The microwave beeps, it's a fanfare for me,
Popcorn bursts forth, a wild jubilee.
With the world at my feet, and chaos my art,
These walls are my audience, my life's funny part.

Forgotten Echoes of Joy

In a room full of socks, chaos takes flight,
Where the cat claims the couch, oh what a sight!
Dust bunnies swirl, doing their dance,
Living room laughter—a whimsical chance.

Tangled up chargers, a puzzle in time,
Uneaten snacks turn into a crime.
The fridge hums a tune, all out of tune,
While shadows perform, under the light of the moon.

The clock on the wall ticks loud as it can,
Reminding me always of my not-so-cool plan.
But in this mad circus of glue and of giggles,
The happiest moments swirl in our wiggles.

So here's to the walls that know all our quirks,
From awkward dance moves to silly old smirks.
In this strange little nest, we live without care,
With echoes of laughter filling the air.

Where Dreams Flourish

In a land of cushions, dreams softly sprout,
Where wild imaginings twirl all about.
A mountain of pillows becomes a great peak,
Pirate ships sailing on the floor, so unique.

The fridge is a treasure chest, full of delight,
With chocolatey secrets hidden from sight.
A conference of spoons gossip while they wait,
Plotting their heist, oh, they just can't be late!

Under the desk, a kingdom takes shape,
With action figures trapped in a brave escape.
And outside the window, a squirrel stands guard,
Scolding the world—but life's not that hard!

So let's toast our pizza to this wacky space,
With a slice of joy, we shall all embrace.
Where creativity flourishes, unbounded and free,
In this haven of giggles, just you and me.

Silhouettes in Stillness

In the corners, dust settles, a cozy affair,
While shadows flicker, dancing without a care.
The chair hums a tune, a creaky old song,
While dreams drape the walls, where we all belong.

Sunbeams spill over, like syrup so sweet,
Taking a stroll on our chocolatey feet.
The couch whispers secrets from flickering nights,
As laughter turns into gentle moonlight fights.

Books loom like giants, with tales yet untold,
Each page a portal to worlds that unfold.
And with every sigh, the walls hold our voice,
In this stitched-up tapestry, we all rejoice.

So here we stay, in this quaint little nook,
Where every old item has memories to cook.
In silhouettes still, we weave and we play,
Creating our magic in a funny ballet.

The Sanctuary We Shape

Amidst the clutter, we craft our own space,
With cereal boxes and a sock puppet race.
The coffee pot laughs, it's seen it all now,
While the microwave sighs, in a glorious bow.

Maps drawn on napkins lead us all astray,
To treasure hunts where the lost items stay.
We giggle at chaos, our favorite pastime,
As we color outside the lines, oh, how sublime!

The window screen shimmers, like a disco ball,
While tangled earbuds perform their strange call.
Fish in the tank eye us with great intrigue,
What wonders await when we all take the league?

So here in our fortress, of fun and delight,
We weave all our tales, both day and night.
In the sanctuary we build, let laughter convene,
With every odd moment, we reign as the queen.

The Warmth of Home

On lazy days, I lounge around,
With snacks and shows, my throne is found.
The cat's my king, ruling with flair,
His judgmental gaze, I strongly bear.

When dishes pile up, it's quite a sight,
I strategize a plan for the night.
Magical powers, I declare with glee,
The art of avoidance, my key victory.

In mismatched socks and a robe that's torn,
I devise a dance, unfit for a morn.
The doorbell rings, and I freeze like a deer,
Pajama-clad ninja, appearing with fear.

Yet laughter echoes in every nook,
In my fortress, I can proudly cook.
With every hiccup and burnt toast disaster,
Home sweet home, it's my joyful master!

Oasis of the Mind

In my little space where sanity reigns,
I find silly thoughts on comfy trains.
Imagination takes flight, it turns out,
Reality's boundaries? I laugh, I shout!

A chair, a desk, a wall with some flair,
A sanctuary made up of utter despair.
The fridge is my muse, the snacks so divine,
A buffet of ideas, where I easily dine.

I type with fervor, my fingers do race,
While cats plot my doom upon my face.
Each blink a reminder of chaotic bliss,
With chaos in order, how could I miss?

So here I dwell, with coffee in hand,
Embarking on journeys far from bland.
In this mental oasis, I crank out the fun,
An adventure awaits, until day is done!

Cocoon of Memories

In the attic, memories float like dust,
Each box a portal, a treasure, a must.
Old photos giggle, giving time a tickle,
The sense of nostalgia makes my heart buckle.

Grandma's old hat, too big for my head,
Looks great in the mirror, a real fashion spread.
The squeak of the floorboards, the shadows that creep,
Tell tales of laughter, secrets I keep.

A fort of blankets, where daydreams reside,
With laughter and whispers, I always confide.
Conversations with ghosts that reside in each frame,
In this cozy cocoon, I play every game.

So here I will linger, lost in the past,
Where the moments are endless, the joy unsurpassed.
In this nest of warmth, I shall always stay,
With memories laughing, come what may!

Enclosed in Peace

The world outside can be quite a fuss,
But here I find tones of soft, sweet trust.
Wrapped in my blanket, a nature retreat,
With snacks arrayed, life is truly sweet.

The clock ticks slowly, like it's on a break,
I sip tea, delighted, for goodness' sake.
Neighbors may grumble, lawn mowers drone,
But I'm just here, in my peaceful zone.

It's quiet chaos, the happiest blend,
Where jokes and giggles always transcend.
In my crystal bubble, life floats like a dream,
As silly thoughts flow, like a bubbly stream.

Though outside can roar, I've built my own wall,
A fortress of laughter, I'll never let fall.
So here I will stay, snug as a bee,
In my quirky haven, endlessly free!

Cradle of Contentment

Within these walls, I'm snug as a bug,
My couch a throne, my coffee a mug.
The socks are scattered, my kingdom's style,
An empire of snacks that makes me smile.

The fridge hums softly, a lullaby sweet,
With leftovers calling, a very fine treat.
The cat's been detained, a furry guard,
While I rule my realm, it's not that hard.

An army of pillows stands tall on my bed,
As I wage my war on sleep, it's said.
Every binge-watched show becomes my own lore,
Battles fought in pajamas, I wage even more.

So here I remain, in my fortress of glee,
With TV as counsel, and takeout for me.
In a world outside wild, I reign, it seems,
As king on the couch, I'll conquer my dreams.

Guarded by Warmth

An abode of laughter, where we freely roam,
Chasing the echoes that turn into home.
My oven's a wizard, baking up cheer,
Where flour fights sugar, and cookies appear.

We're barricaded nicely in cozy attire,
With a blanket fort made, now that's pure desire.
Kids hide in corners, like ninja on strike,
While parents sip tea, just passing the mic.

The vacuum's a dragon, it roars through the halls,
As we battle its noise, we're ready to brawl.
The dog's chasing shadows, a comedic sight,
In a land of chaos, everything's right.

So let's turn the noise into laughter, my friend,
Our fortress of warmth, on it we can depend.
Where everyday antics are the best kind of art,
In our little sanctuary, we each play a part.

Enigma of Enclosure

Within these boundaries, the riddle remains,
Why do socks vanish? It's driving me insane!
The walls are confessions, secrets they tell,
Of clumsy moves and coffee spills that fell.

Here laughter is currency, joy's got a fee,
My closet holds treasures, like a cat's mystery.
My roommate's strange dance moves are rather sublime,
We practice our quirks, it's a real good time.

This space is an enigma, a puzzle of fun,
With puzzles now solved, our kooky life's begun.
From pizza boxes to dance-offs at night,
The strange little moments make everything right.

So we embrace mayhem, it's our favorite art,
In this whimsically wired, sumptuously smart.
Around these odd walls, our laughter can soar,
A riddle of friendship, we couldn't ask for more.

The Spaces We Own

Our walls tell a story, a canvas of mirth,
With colorful chaos, the jazz of our hearth.
The chairs are forever lost in a war,
Each one claiming a throne, just plotting for more.

From dance parties chaotic to awkwardly posed,
We laugh till we cry, oh how we've dozed.
The fridge is our oracle, snacks whisper fate,
Telling tales of late nights, we laugh and relate.

With laughter as armor, we're ready to play,
Each nook holds a memory that won't fade away.
In our cozy dominion, we rule with delight,
Creating wise legends in the soft, golden light.

So here's to the mischief, the joy that abounds,
In every little corner, where pure fun surrounds.
We craft our adventures, the stories we'll weave,
In this quirky palace — oh, we won't leave!

Heart's Fortress

In my cozy nook, a cat takes a nap,
While I craft my dreams, all cozy and zapped.
With snacks on the side, a feast just for me,
I swear this fortress, is my grand jubilee.

Outside the wild world makes a ruckus, no doubt,
But here I'm a king, with my dog in clout.
We laugh at the chaos that raves at the door,
With slippers for armor, we're ready for more!

Curled up with a book, I snicker and grin,
As I sip my hot cocoa, I savor the win.
This fortress of mine holds the tickles of cheer,
Not a soul here to judge, so I'll dance without fear!

In laughter we twirl, in safety we thrive,
While outside whispers, 'Are they really alive?'
With walls that embrace, in mischief we play,
My heart's little castle, where goofiness stays!

The Bonds of Space

Inside these four walls, mischief takes flight,
Where socks go missing, a comical sight.
I ponder the mysteries of missing left shoes,
While munching on popcorn, I've nothing to lose.

The walls seem to chuckle, with echoes of fun,
As my couch becomes mine, my rule has begun.
I lead a crusade of fluff and of fluff,
Against dust bunnies plotting, it's all rather tough.

The fridge hums a tune, it knows all my traits,
It holds midnight snacks, my ever-rare mates.
Uninvited, they say, 'You really should share!'
But why would I when munching's a solo affair?

Their wise, silent whispers tell tales of the day,
While I chuckle and nod, as I feign dismay.
These bonds of my space sit snug as they stay,
In my silly little kingdom, I'm ruler, hooray!

Wrapped in Quietude

Bathed in sunshine, I lounge with delight,
As roaming dust motes dance, oh what a sight!
Wrapped like a burrito, on my couch, I dwell,
In this silence, I giggle, all's right in my shell.

With walls as my audience, I belt out a tune,
Each off-key note strikes like a comical boon.
The paint starts to chip, yet they clap for my show,
In this sanctuary, I'm free to let go!

My slippers are heroes, they keep out the cold,
In this star-studded living room, laughter unfolds.
Like a marshmallow pillow, I bounce with a cheer,
Wrapped in my haven, who needs a frontier?

The clock ticks beside me, not missing a beat,
While I plot the next chapter of napping elite.
Quietude's a canvas, with colors galore,
Where joy paints my laughter, forever and more!

Within These Sheltered Secrets

Behind closed doors, where whispers reside,
Lies a kingdom of giggles that we all abide.
Secret handshakes, and jokes caught on air,
Within these walls, we've no burdens to bear.

My room is a fortress, of blankets and fun,
Where I wield a remote like a toy-made-gun.
With snacks piled high, a negotiator's dream,
This laughter-lined space reigns supreme, it would seem!

Tucked up in corners, we plot and we scheme,
While the laundry hampers hold a grumpy regime.
We laugh as we dodge that daunting ol' chore,
In this hideaway, I'm neither rich nor poor!

In silliness wrapped, our secrets, they bubble,
While outside the world rumbles, perhaps in trouble.
Inside, we find joy, amid cushions and cheer,
In these sheltered moments, we hold our hearts dear!

The Nest of Dreams

In my little cocoon, there's a sock on the floor,
A party for dust bunnies, who could ask for more?
The couch is my throne, with crumbs for a feast,
My cat's the best jester, and I am the beast.

Walls whisper secrets, while I binge and recline,
They nudge me to snack—oh, what a divine sign!
My kingdom of chaos, where laughter runs free,
With delightful absurdities, just my cat and me.

Floating on cushions, I nap without care,
Dreams weave around me like my old, frayed chair.
The fridge hums a tune, joining in on the fun,
In my nest of oddities, life's never done.

So let's raise a toast, to the clutter we share,
To the echoes of giggles that float through the air.
In the haven of nonsense, all silliness thrives,
This nest holds the magic of simple lives.

Walls that Listen

In the quiet of corner, the walls take a peek,
They hear all my musings—oh boy, do they speak!
With a creak and a sigh, they understood my jest,
As I plan my next 'cooking' which is always a mess.

God bless the quaint tiles, they hide all the stains,
With stories of puddles and laughable gains.
Each bump in the wall knows my funniest fables,
As I dance in pajamas, defying all labels.

Every tick of the clock sings a rhythmic delight,
While my fridge hums along in a symphonic night.
The curtains are snickering, my plants chuckle too,
In this warm little box, there's love that rings true.

So here's to the spaces where giggles ignite,
Where the paint knows my secrets, and holds them so tight.
Let's toast to these walls, my companions so loyal,
In this cozy abode, life's a playful royal.

Embracing the Stillness

Amidst all the stillness, my thoughts start to race,
In the blanket fort I've built, I bow out of the chase.
A fortress of cushions where time stands quite still,
And the world fades away—oh what a thrill!

The clock on the mantle has lost all its grind,
Who needs all the chaos? It's peace that I find.
With snacks in my pocket, and socks mismatched,
I lounge like a king, in a robe that's unmatched.

Every little rustle is music to me,
The world might be busy, but I've found my spree.
With popcorn explosions and giggles galore,
I'm embracing the stillness, who could want more?

In this hush of the room, humor dances around,
As I slip into daydreams, profound yet unbound.
Tucked in the corner, my laughter takes flight,
In this home of serenity, I'm lost in delight.

Boundless Intimacy

Oh, the charm of this space where the chaos abounds,
Surrounded by treasures—both silly and sound.
My slippers are mismatched, my laundry, a sight,
But we're all in this together, what pure, goofy delight!

Every hour is filled with my quirky pursuits,
Like mastering the art of wearing rain boots.
The walls wrap me snug, a hug that won't fade,
As I twirl with my dog, in this wacky parade.

Laughter stains the corners, and spills on the floor,
My pet's judgemental glare? Well, who could ask for more!
With every shared moment, the silliness gleams,
In this boundless abyss, we weave our wild dreams.

So raise up a glass to the quirky and bright,
To the strange little wonders that fill up the night.
In this petite kingdom, we gather and chime,
A crew of the silly, we laugh out of time.

www.ingramcontent.com/pod-product-compliance
Lightning Source LLC
Chambersburg PA
CBHW070002300426
43661CB00141B/130